IN AND AROUND
LONDON

WESTMINSTER

ABOVE: The Houses of
Parliament on the banks of
the River Thames. The Union
flag is hoisted on Victoria
Tower when Parliament
is in session.

The heart of Britain's power is in essence based in the Houses of Parliament although the country has no written constitution. Known correctly as the New Palace of Westminster, this imposing home to democracy stands proudly beside the River Thames and the Lords and the Commons regularly meet to debate and pass laws. Edward the Confessor originally established a royal home – the Old Palace – to keep a watchful eye on the building of the nearby Westminster Abbey. The palace was later used to assemble the King's Council and the Great Parliament of 1265. It was destroyed by a devastating fire in 1834, portrayed in J. M. W. Turner's painting, *The Burning of the Houses of Lords and Commons, October 16, 1834*. The New Palace of Westminster was rebuilt in Gothic style by leading architect Sir Charles Barry to reflect the important work going on within its walls.

The day-to-day business of government takes place in the green Chamber of the House of Commons, with the Government sitting on the left and the Opposition on the right. The Speaker keeps order during debates from his chair in the middle. The 650 Members of Parliament (MPs) are elected by the people and work here, although there is only enough room for two thirds to be seated at any one time! Destroyed in 1941 during an air raid, the chamber was rebuilt with less flamboyance but more intimacy. The historic silver gilt mace represents the authority delegated to the Commons by the Sovereign, a sign of privilege and power. It is always placed on the centre table to mark that parliamentary proceedings are in progress.

A light shines from the top of the 95.7-metre (314-ft high) Clock Tower to signify when Parliament is in session. Better known as Big Ben, the name refers to its mighty 13.5-tonne bell whose chimes are familiar around the world and broadcast by the BBC.

BELOW: The Clock Tower which houses Big Ben. It is not certain whether the bell was named after champion boxer, Benjamin Caunt, or the First Commissioner of Works, Sir Benjamin Hall.

BELOW LEFT: The mighty 13.5 tonne hour bell called Big Ben. It was cast on Saturday 10 April 1858, with the first chime rung in situ on 31 May 1859.

RIGHT: Members of
Parliament, Lords and the
Monarch come together for
the State Opening of
Parliament in the Upper
Chamber. The Queen
delivers her speech detailing
the government's
programme, and Parliament
is declared open.
•

The House of Lords or Upper Chamber is a fine example of Gothic-style architecture and sumptuously decorated in rich opulent red. Its role is generally acknowledged to be complementary to the Commons and acts as a revising chamber for many of the more important and controversial bills. The Lord Chancellor presides by sitting on an ancient woolsack, dating back to Edward III. It houses the monarch's throne and was the target for the 1605 Gunpowder Plot to blow up Parliament and King James I. William Rufus, the son of William the Conqueror, built the vast Westminster Hall, completed in 1099, and is the only surviving part of the original Palace. Charles I was tried and sentenced to death here during the Civil War. More recently, former Prime Minister Sir Winston Churchill and the Queen Mother lay in state here.

For the State Opening of Parliament The Queen arrives at the arch underneath Victoria Tower. She proceeds into the Lords and her representative, Black Rod, is sent to the Commons, where the door is traditionally slammed in his face to exclude the monarch from meddling in Commons' business. He must knock three times to gain admittance.

BELOW: The Cenotaph memorial, designed by Sir Edwin Lutyens and erected in 1920. On Remembrance Sunday, a service commemorates those lost in war and wreaths of red poppies are laid. A two-minute silence is also observed.

•

LEFT: The official entrance to Buckingham Palace, Horse Guards is guarded by two mounted troopers of the Household Cavalry from 11am till 4pm daily (10am on Sunday).

•

RIGHT: The spartan living quarters in the Cabinet War Rooms at Whitehall are preserved just as they were left in 1945.

•

Once used as the official residence of Tudor and Stuart Monarchs, Whitehall was destroyed by fire in 1698 only leaving the Banqueting Hall intact. The official residence of the Prime Minister is at 10, Downing Street, on the boundary where the palace used to stand, with government offices now occupying both sides of the street. Diplomat, spy and property developer George Downing provided the street with its name and his portrait hangs in the entrance hall. During the Second World War secret government meetings between Prime Minister Winston Churchill and the Cabinet were held in underground concrete-covered Cabinet War Rooms in King Charles Street. Visitors can see them as they were at that time. Nearby Tate Britain houses a magnificent national collection of British art, from 1500 to the present day.

ABOVE: An entire wing at Tate Britain, on the north banks of the Thames at Millbank, displays paintings by J.M.W. Turner.

•

RIGHT: Westminster Cathedral was completed in 1903 and, although the interior is incomplete, it contains fine marblework and mosaics.

•

Westminster Cathedral, designed by John Francis Bentley, stands on a former prison site and was built with 12 million red bricks and white Portland stone. The striped Byzantine style and the 87-metre (285ft) campanile (St Edward's Tower) marks the building from afar. A high cross contains a relic of the True Cross. The cathedral's nave, the widest in England, measures 18 metres (60ft) across. Inside, works of art include Eric Gill's reliefs of the Stations of the Cross.

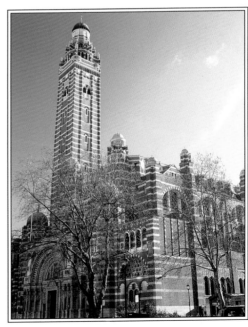

WESTMINSTER ABBEY

Every coronation since William the Conqueror has taken place in glorious Westminster Abbey. It has seen many royal funerals, including those of Diana, Princess of Wales and the Queen Mother. West Monastery or Westminster sits to the west of the city of London and has been a place of worship since AD960. The abbey was re-founded by Edward the Confessor but most of what is visible today was built under the auspices of Henry III, between 1220 and 1272. The abbey's imposing exterior has remained largely unchanged since the Reformation.

ABOVE: Westminster Abbey's nave with its many chandeliers, viewed from the quire screen, looking towards the west door.

•

LEFT: Oscar Romero, Archbishop of San Salvador and human rights campaigner, is one of the ten statues of Martyrs of the 20th Century over the west door.

•

RIGHT: Westminster Abbey's west front towers were completed by Nicholas Hawksmoor from original designs by Sir Christopher Wren, and were built in 1745.

•

BELOW: William Wordsworth is commemorated in Poets' Corner together with many other writers including Charles Dickens and William Shakespeare.

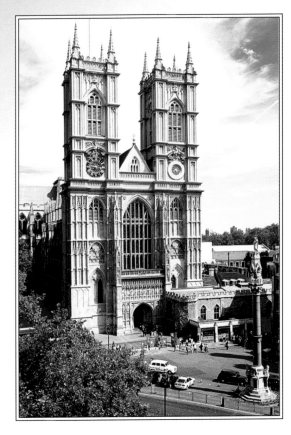

The west front features the statues of Martyrs of the 20th Century, including civil rights leader Martin Luther King. Unveiled in 1998, they nestle in existing spaces that were never filled, above the four figures of Truth, Justice, Mercy and Peace. A statue of Queen Anne stands in front of the west door. The great west window spreads light over the nave which, at 31 metres (103ft) tall, is the highest medieval Gothic vault in England and took 150 years to build. Huge flying buttresses spread the weight and support the structure. Sixteen exquisite Waterford crystal chandeliers mark the abbey's 900-year anniversary in 1965.

The Lady Chapel (Henry VII's Chapel), built in the Perpendicular Gothic style, is a wonder of the medieval world because of its beautiful craftsmanship and is the burial place

for Henry VII. The elaborate bronze gates are decorated with Tudor badges and were probably made by Thomas Ducheman. The choir stalls were completed in 1512.

Although not originally intended as a burial place for writers, Poets' Corner has become the resting place for many famous authors, playwrights and poets; the first to be buried here were Geoffrey Chaucer, author of *The Canterbury Tales,* (*c.* 1343–1400) and poet Edmund Spenser (1553–99) who wrote *The Fairie Queene.*

WESTMINSTER ABBEY

LEFT: The Lady Chapel (Henry VII's Chapel) is surrounded by coloured banners, crests and mantlings of knights, which adorn the 16th-century wooden stalls. Beneath the seats are beautifully carved misericords, while above is the delicate fan-vaulted ceiling.

In 1301 Edward I ordered the making of the oak Coronation Chair, sited just outside St Edward's Chapel, to surround the Scottish Stone of Scone he had captured five years earlier. Some of its original gilt and delicate patterns have faded over the years and it intriguingly now bears the hallmarks of people's carved signatures. It has been used in nearly every sovereign's coronation since 1308 including the coronation of Queen Elizabeth II in 1953. The stone was returned to Scotland in 1996, some 700 years after its capture.

St Edward's Chapel houses the magnificent golden shrine of St Edward the Confessor and is situated just east of the sanctuary, containing the tombs of five kings and four queens, including Henry V. The chapel is shielded by a 15th-century stone screen ornately carved with scenes from St Edward's life. Originally it was made in three parts: a decorated stone base, a gold container for the saint's coffin and an overhead canopy, which could be raised to reveal the golden shrine or lowered to protect it. For centuries worshippers left precious offerings to enrich the shrine and it was held in such esteem the sick often stayed nearby overnight in the hope of a miracle cure.

ABOVE: Westminster Abbey from Dean's Yard, a pretty green overlooking the abbey, and a quiet contemplative place to enjoy the historic view.

•

RIGHT: Marble marking the Grave of the Unknown Warrior was transported from Belgium, near to First World War battlegrounds. It is the only tomb set in the floor that you cannot walk over.

•

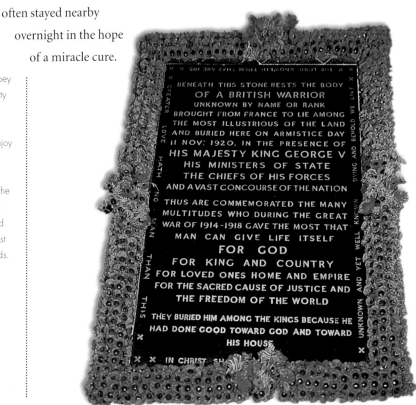

BENEATH THIS STONE RESTS THE BODY OF A BRITISH WARRIOR UNKNOWN BY NAME OR RANK BROUGHT FROM FRANCE TO LIE AMONG THE MOST ILLUSTRIOUS OF THE LAND AND BURIED HERE ON ARMISTICE DAY 11 NOV: 1920, IN THE PRESENCE OF HIS MAJESTY KING GEORGE V HIS MINISTERS OF STATE THE CHIEFS OF HIS FORCES AND A VAST CONCOURSE OF THE NATION

THUS ARE COMMEMORATED THE MANY MULTITUDES WHO DURING THE GREAT WAR OF 1914-1918 GAVE THE MOST THAT MAN CAN GIVE LIFE ITSELF FOR GOD FOR KING AND COUNTRY FOR LOVED ONES HOME AND EMPIRE FOR THE SACRED CAUSE OF JUSTICE AND THE FREEDOM OF THE WORLD

THEY BURIED HIM AMONG THE KINGS BECAUSE HE HAD DONE GOOD TOWARD GOD AND TOWARD HIS HOUSE

X X IN CHRIST SH

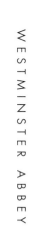

LEFT: The Tomb of Edward the Confessor has recesses in which to pray. Dismantled in 1540, it was reassembled and the canopy has been restored.

•

BELOW: Sovereigns are crowned in the Coronation Chair, which was made in 1301 on the orders of Edward I.

•

The Grave of the Unknown Warrior provides a moving tribute to those men who died unidentified in the First World War. The body of an unknown soldier brought back from the battlefields is buried beneath the inscribed black marble stone close to the west door. The words 'They buried him among the Kings,' are from the Bible.

RIGHT: St Martin-in-the-Fields's influence extends abroad as it has become the model in America for Colonial-style churches. Unusually, it has a royal box to the left of the altar. It also houses the London Brass Rubbing Centre.

BELOW: Trafalgar Square's fountains were substantially remodelled in 1939 by Sir Edwin Lutyens and feature mermen, mermaids and dolphins in bronze.

TRAFALGAR SQUARE

Trafalgar Square is one of London's great meeting places, especially in warm weather when the fountains prove a great attraction. Created as a monument to British naval power, it commemorates Nelson's victory over Napoleon in the momentous Battle of Trafalgar in 1805 when Britain ruled the waves and almost a quarter of the planet. The neo-classical design by John Nash provided a dramatic open space and linked the major routes across London. It was remodelled in 1840 by Sir Charles Barry to include the northern terrace and steps. During the summer of 2003, the north side of the square was pedestrianized.

Curiously, Barry objected to Nelson's Column, but was overruled and construction of the imposing 51-metre (167ft) column went ahead, taking three years to build. High above the square the granite statue of Admiral Lord Nelson stands proudly at the top, looking towards the River Thames and Parliament. At the base, bronze plaques cast from cannons depict scenes from Nelson's battles at St Vincent, the Nile, the bombardment of Copenhagen and also his death at Trafalgar. Four magnificent bronze lions on plinths, sculpted by Sir Edwin Landseer, stand on guard. In the north-eastern corner of Trafalgar Square is the church of St Martin-in-the-Fields, the oldest building in the area, once so popular that pews had to be rented. The church, designed by renowned Scottish architect James Gibbs, was completed in 1726 and was so named because the area was beyond the city boundaries and surrounded by green fields. Charles II's mistress, Nell Gwynne, is buried here and the crypts were once used as air raid shelters during the Second World War. In the crypt there is a brass rubbing centre, bookshop and café.

LEFT: Stonemasons had dinner on the column's base before Nelson's statue was put on. The lions were an afterthought, added 25 years later.

•

BELOW LEFT: The people of Oslo, Norway have donated a Christmas tree every year since 1947 as thanks for Britain's help in the Second World War, sheltering the Norwegian royal family.

•

RIGHT: Despite objections to the vast number of pigeons in Trafalgar Square, they remain an irresistible attraction.

•

BELOW: Pearly Kings and Queens, representing east London tradesmen and women, gather in St Martin-in-the-Fields.

•

The 'Pearlies' are costermongers, street sellers of fruit and vegetables whose tradition of dressing in clothes covered in pearly buttons was started by the orphan Henry Croft. At the age of 13, Henry obtained a job as a road sweeper and wanted to help those less fortunate than himself so, to raise money, he swept the market streets and collected pearl buttons that had fallen off people's clothes. He sewed them on to his cap and suit. On the first Sunday in October, the Pearly Kings and Queens hold a Harvest Festival service at St Martin-in-the-Fields, where the Pearly princesses take bouquets of vegetables.

TRAFALGAR SQUARE

On the north side of Trafalgar Square lies the National Gallery which contains one of the most extensive painting collections in the world. George IV used his influence with the government to buy 38 renowned paintings for the start of a national collection. European art dates from the 13th century to the 19th century, including Van Gogh's *Sunflowers*, Velazquez's *Rokeby Venus* and works by Titian, Rembrandt, Constable and Monet.

LEFT: *The Toilet of Venus 'The Rokeby Venus'*, painted in 1649 by Diego Velazquez, forms part of the remarkable collection at the National Gallery.

•

BELOW: A portrait of maritime hero, Admiral Lord Nelson in the National Portrait Gallery, painted by Lemuel Francis Abbott in 1797.

•

The National Portrait Gallery, in St Martin's Place, contains more than 10,000 portraits of the best-known faces in Britain, from politicians and sportsmen to writers and heroes. There is a cartoon of Henry VIII and paintings of wives, along with the earliest portrait of Shakespeare, and atio Nelson together with his mistress, Emma Hamilton. rooftop restaurant has wonderful views over Trafalgar re and Whitehall.

Admiralty Arch, more modern than much he surrounding area, was commis- oned by Queen Victoria's son King Edward VII. Designed by Sir Aston Webb, it has become an important city landmark. There are five arches, which mark the start of The Mall and the route to Buckingham Palace.

Known originally as Buckingham House, Buckingham Palace is the official London home of The Queen and was built for John, first Duke of Buckingham in 1702. Its palatial character was created over time by successive monarchs and royal architects including John Nash. Queen Victoria became the first sovereign to live at the Palace and an east wing was completed in 1847 to accommodate her growing family. The Palace is now used for both state occasions and as The Queen's private residence. The opulent State Rooms (open in August and September) are entered through Nash's Grand Hall and feature his romantic three-flight Grand Staircase with a gilded balustrade, costing £3,900 in 1830. State Visits are held in the State Ballroom, where many lavish banquets are held. Around 300 people work at the Palace, from officers of the Royal Household to domestic staff.

BUCKINGHAM PALACE

RIGHT: The Gold State Coach with The Queen inside, parading through London's streets during The Queen's Golden Jubilee celebrations in 2002. It can be seen at the Royal Mews.

Every morning from April to the end of July (alternate days during autumn and winter) military precision and a blaze of colour mark the Changing of the Guard, known officially as Guard Mounting. Visitors can see soldiers in real bearskin hats and red tunics patrolling Buckingham Palace. At the front of the palace, the Queen Victoria Memorial, designed in 1901 by Sir Aston Webb, is the centrepiece for his Mall plan. The seated sculpture by Sir Thomas Brock is surrounded by allegorical figures representing Victorian virtues, such as Truth, Constancy and Courage.

ABOVE: The Queen Victoria Memorial, which sits on the island in front of Buckingham Palace, is Edward VII's tribute from a son to his mother.

LEFT: The soldiers who guard Buckingham Palace perform the traditional Changing of the Guard ceremony wearing full military regalia.

BELOW: The magnificent
Trooping the Colour
ceremony takes place on
The Queen's official birthday
in June. It begins at
Buckingham Palace and
journeys down The Mall to
Horse Guards.

Home to the Royal coaches and their horses, the Royal Mews stables and coach houses were designed by leading architect John Nash in 1825. The 1761 Gold State Coach built for George III, the 1910 Glass Coach – used for nearly all royal weddings – and royal landaus are kept and looked after here, together with Rolls Royce Phantoms and Daimlers, the Royal Family's favourite cars. Clarence House, built in 1827 for William IV, became home to the Queen Mother until her death in 2002. She bequeathed it to Prince Charles and he oversaw extensive renovations the following summer. Some rooms are now open to the public during the summer for viewing. Displays include the Queen Mother's extensive collection of art and furniture, examples of Fabergé, English porcelain and silver, and works by John Piper.

LEFT: The Throne Room at Buckingham Palace with thrones used by The Queen and the Duke of Edinburgh during her Coronation in 1953. Other sovereigns' thrones sit majestically around the room.

•

BELOW: The Queen's Gallery contains priceless paintings and works of art and is one of the finest collections in the world.

The Queen's Gallery houses one of the best art collections in the world, including paintings by many Old Masters such as Leonardo da Vinci. Also on display are textiles, furniture, jewellery and decorative art. The Throne Room's ornate ceiling is illuminated by seven glass and gilt bronze chandeliers that are two hundred years old and it is here that The Queen receives addresses on formal occasions. Nearby St James's Palace was built on the site of a former leper hospital built by Henry VIII. Its impressive gatehouse is one of the most recognizable Tudor sites in London and it was until recently home to Prince Charles and his household.

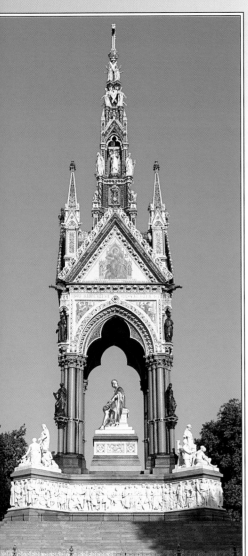

Prince Albert died from typhoid aged just 41, and his widow, Queen Victoria, honoured his memory with the Albert Memorial. It took 15 years to complete and stands 55 metres (175ft) high. Based on a medieval market cross with almost 200 figures, Prince Albert is seen holding a copy of the catalogue for the 1851 Great Exhibition, which he helped organize and which inspired the creation of museums around Kensington. The statue was gilded again in 1998 after being blacked out with paint during the Second World War.

A cornucopia of ceramics, furniture, fashion, glass, jewellery, metalwork, photographs, sculpture, textiles and paintings makes the Victoria and Albert Museum one of the world's greatest museums of art and design with 11 kilometres (7 miles) of galleries to explore. Opened as the Department of Oriental Art in the Museum of Manufactures in Marlborough House in 1852, it moved to South Kensington in 1857 and was renamed in 1899 by Queen Victoria in memory of her husband. The exterior by Sir Aston Webb has 32 sculptures.

KENSINGTON

ABOVE: The Albert Memorial is a tribute from a bereaved Queen Victoria to her husband.

•

RIGHT: *The Three Graces* by Antonio Canova 1757-1822, at the Victoria and Albert Museum.

•

It is home to 3,000 years' worth of amazing artefacts from many of the world's richest cultures. Highlights include the breathtaking Cast Courts with extraordinary reproductions of priceless international works, the national collection of paintings by Constable, the largest collection of Italian Renaissance sculpture outside Italy and the stunning British Galleries, illustrating the history of Britain through the country's art and design.

The Royal Albert Hall, constructed using iron and glass, was designed by engineer Francis Fowke. Inspired by Roman amphitheatres, it was completed in 1871. The colourful Promenade Concerts ('Proms') take place here every summer.

BELOW: The Royal Albert Hall is ringed by a frieze in praise of the arts and sciences.

•

ABOVE: The Natural History
Museum aims to explain
how the world works and
captivates both children and
adults alike.

•

RIGHT: Sir George
Frampton's 1912 statue in
Kensington Gardens of
J.M. Barrie's Peter Pan, the
boy who never grew up,
playing music to animals
and fairies below.

•

A public park and a favourite with children for over 150 years, Kensington Gardens now contains a children's playground in memory of Diana, Princess of Wales. The gardens include Frampton's statue of Peter Pan, the boy who never grew up. Kensington is now a centre for museums following on from the 1851 Great Exhibition. Prince Albert, Queen Victoria's consort, used the Great Exhibition to publicize British science and technology and, as a result, the government set up a Science & Art Department, which established the South Kensington Museum in 1857, from which the present Science Museum evolved. Now there are 300 years of science in over 40 galleries and 2,000 hands-on exhibits to experience, from the first automatic calculator to Apollo 10. The 1881 Natural History Museum, designed by Alfred Waterhouse, holds many answers to the secrets of life on earth with a simulated earthquake and eruption, and life-size robotic dinosaurs.

BLOOMSBURY & BAKER STREET

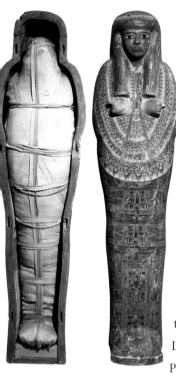

Bloomsbury, a wonderful mix of Georgian squares, was once renowned for writers and intellectuals such as Virginia Woolf, George Bernard Shaw and T.S. Eliot living there in the early 1900s, who were known as the Bloomsbury Set. Britain's largest collection of treasures is housed in the British Museum, which was opened in 1759 and contains six-and-a-half million exhibits. In recent years it has undergone major reconstruction and its inner court, designed by Sir Norman Foster, is now covered in a steel-and-glass roof, creating London's first indoor square. The star attractions include the Elgin Marbles, taken by Lord Elgin to London from the Parthenon in Athens in 1801; the Rosetta Stone, the key that allowed scholars to decipher hieroglyphics; Sutton Hoo, an Anglo-Saxon wooden burial ship, and Egyptian mummies.

In 1997, taking more than 15 years to build, the British Library, designed by Colin St John Wilson, moved to Euston Road. The library contains a copy of nearly every book printed in Britain, and there are three exhibition galleries. Documents include the Magna Carta (1215); a copy of the Gutenberg Bible; Shakespeare's First Folio and a notebook of Leonardo da Vinci's.

One of Britain's foremost authors, Charles Dickens, lived at 48 Doughty Street from April 1837 to December 1839. The house has now been converted into the Charles Dickens Museum, with 11 memorabilia-crammed rooms.

In the north-east corner of Regent's Park lies London Zoo, the home of the Zoological Society of London. It places great emphasis on conservation, while its Penguin Pool, Aviary and children's enclosure are very popular.

LEFT: Egyptian Mummies at the British Museum, the oldest public museum in the world.

•

BELOW: Diana, a black-and-white ruffed lemur, being playful at London Zoo which has over 600 species of animal.

•

RIGHT: The Sherlock Holmes
Museum recreates 221b
Baker Street. You can even
buy a deerstalker hat just like
the famous detective's.

Madame Tussaud's waxworks has long been one of London's top attractions. Visitors can meet, touch and be photographed with some of the most famous faces in the world. There are life-like models of celebrities and stars from the movies, politics and royalty. During the French revolution, Marie Grosholtz, who later married François Tussaud, prepared death masks for guillotine victims. She spent 33 years touring Britain before settling at a museum site in 1835 not far from the present building. The Chamber of Horrors harks back to the grisly beginnings of the museum and uses wax figures to recreate gruesome crimes and murders. The grand finale is the 'Spirit Of London', an electric ride with commentary.

Near by, the fictional character Sherlock Holmes untangled many a tricky crime while living at 221b Baker Street, as told by the author, Sir Arthur Conan Doyle. The Sherlock Holmes Museum recreates his home, complete with an actor playing the detective's loyal friend Dr Watson.

BELOW: Dancing with Kylie Minogue is one of the star attractions at Madame Tussaud's.

Begun around 1078, with a moat for extra security, the Tower of London was a way for King William I to secure England's most powerful city, its armoury and its jewels. Previously the tallest and best-defended building in London, today it remains remarkably intact and houses a wealth of treasure such as the Crown Jewels and a glimpse into a past way of life both for kings and queens – and traitors.

THE TOWER OF LONDON

BELOW: The imposing Tower of London. The last prisoner incarcerated was Rudolph Hess, Hitler's second-in-command. The magnificent Crown Jewels are still protected here.

The Chief Yeoman Warder, dressed in a traditional scarlet coat and Tudor bonnet, has responsibility for locking the Tower every night. New Yeoman Warders are sworn in on Tower Green where they take an oath of allegiance to the reigning monarch. The new recruits join other Yeoman Warders, and their health is toasted from a ceremonial punch bowl.

LEFT: The Chief Yeoman Warder oversees security at the Tower in an elaborate ceremony dating back to the 14th century.

RIGHT: The original single entrance on the south side of the White Tower was reached by an external staircase because there were no doors at ground level.

•

BELOW: The ravens are fed on a diet of raw meat and bird formula biscuits soaked in blood each day. They are also partial to an egg plus the occasional rabbit!

•

There are around 40 Yeoman Warders at the Tower, acting as guides telling stories about past exploits in the tower as well as performing ceremonial duties. They are now selected from among the military for their long service and good conduct. They are known as 'beefeaters' because it's said they were lucky enough to dine on meat even during times of beef shortage.

Giving the castle its name at the centre of the courtyard is the four-turreted White Tower, started in 1078 as a stronghold to house the Royal Armoury, but not completed until 1097. It was later ordered by Henry III to be whitewashed inside and out. Towering 27 metres (90ft) high, the white Normandy Caen stone walls are up to 4.6 metres (15ft) thick. The foundations were laid under the direction of Gundulf, Bishop of Rochester, a famous builder of castles and churches. It contains a 12-metre (40-ft) deep well and displays some of the Royal Armouries, along with instruments of torture and punishment. Another part of the Royal Armouries is now housed in Leeds.

Charles II's astronomer, John Flamsteed, complained ravens were interfering with his star-gazing from the White Tower. The King ordered the birds to be destroyed but was soon warned of the consequences, for legend has it that if the ravens leave the Tower, the kingdom will fall. The birds, which live for up to 25 years and are cared for by the Ravenmaster, were allowed to stay after having their wings clipped to prevent escape.

The Bloody Tower holds many dark secrets, most notably that of the innocent sons and heirs of Edward IV, known as the 'Little Princes', who were probably smothered inside the tower in 1483 on the orders of their uncle, later crowned Richard III. A chest containing the remains of the two children was found in 1674 and then re-buried in the peaceful surroundings of Innocents' Corner, Westminster Abbey. Sir Walter Raleigh, imprisoned by James I, spent 13 years in the Bloody Tower. The now bricked-up Traitors' Gate was the wide river entrance at St Thomas's Tower and is the point at which prisoners, accused of treason, knew they would never return, as they were en route to their execution.

ABOVE: The Bloody Tower was built during the reign of Henry III (1216–72) as a water-gate for the Tower. It had an arched opening in the wall leading directly into the River Thames.

•

BELOW: Traitors' Gate, the dreaded entrance to the Tower for prisoners, which sealed their fate.

•

The Chapel of St John the Evangelist in the White Tower is built from French stone. Noblemen, before being invested as knights in the ceremony of the Order of the Bath, would keep overnight vigil in the chapel. In 1503 the body of Elizabeth of York, wife of Henry VII lay in state here.

The Crown Jewels, worn in coronations and other ceremonial events, have been used by every English king and queen. They have been kept at the Tower since the 1300s. In 1671 'Colonel' Thomas Blood, in a daring raid, grabbed the crown, orb and sceptre and made a dash towards Tower Wharf, where he and his cohorts were arrested. The priceless jewels are now kept in the Waterloo Barracks where visitors can see the largest quality cut diamond in the world, the First Star of Africa, weighing over 530 carats, set in the head of the Sceptre with the Cross.

ABOVE RIGHT: The priceless Crown Jewels and the Imperial State Crown as worn by The Queen at every State Opening of Parliament. It has 2,868 diamonds, 17 sapphires, 11 emeralds, 5 rubies and 273 pearls.

•

RIGHT: Part of the medieval palace, the upper chamber of the Wakefield Tower was built for Henry III between 1220 and 1240.

•

Wakefield Tower, the second largest tower, contains a magnificent raised throne copied from the Coronation Chair in Westminster Abbey. Two of Henry VIII's wives, Anne Boleyn and Catherine Howard, were beheaded at Tower Green. It is now surrounded by buildings and used by those who live and work at the Tower. Catherine Howard, Lady Jane Grey and Sir Thomas More are buried in the Chapel Royal of St Peter ad Vincula.

Every night, in an age-old tradition known as the Ceremony of the Keys, the Yeoman Warders are joined by a military guard to ensure the safety of the Tower. A sentry demands, 'Halt! Who goes there?' The Chief Warder boldly replies, 'The Keys.' The outer gates are locked and the keys taken to the Resident Governor of the Tower.

Today gun salutes can still be heard at the western end of Tower Wharf, which had the ceremonial role of providing the landing place for royalty and dignitaries as they entered the city. Sixty-two guns are fired for The Queen's birthday and 41 for the State Opening of Parliament, or when a foreign head of state visits.

ABOVE:
The traditional Ceremony of the Keys where the Tower is secured for the night against intruders.

•

LEFT: A gun salute on Tower Wharf from powerful 25-pounder guns, held on royal birthdays and important national events, such as the State Opening of Parliament.

•

ST PAUL'S CATHEDRAL

FAR RIGHT: Sir Christopher Wren's elegant dome, chosen in place of a spire, crowns St Paul's Cathedral as a glorious landmark on London's skyline.

•

RIGHT: The quire and high altar were the first part of the cathedral to be built and consecrated. The choir and clergy sit here during services.

•

BELOW RIGHT: Great Paul, at 17 tonnes the largest bell in England, sits in the south-west tower of St Paul's. It is tolled each day at 1pm.

•

Standing nobly amid London's skyline, St Paul's Cathedral has survived for over 400 years and endures as one of the most popular and moving sights in the city. It was started in 1675, 15 years after the Great Fire destroyed four-fifths of the city of London. The first Christian cathedral on this site dates back to 604 and Sir Christopher Wren's design is the fifth on this spot. Miraculously, it survived the Blitz during the Second World War and is still used for royal weddings, state funerals (like that of prime minister Sir Winston Churchill in 1965), tributes and special services of thanks.

In the north quire aisle, Henry Moore's evocative sculpture *Mother and Child* represents three different stages of motherhood. The quire and high altar contain choir stalls with ornate carvings of cherubs, fruits and garlands by craftsman Grinling Gibbons who also worked at Windsor Castle and Hampton Court. He made the cathedral's organ case, which houses the instrument once played by Handel and Mendelssohn. The latter played for so long, cathedral staff had to let the wind out of the instrument to make him stop!

On the south side is the Bishop's throne, or *cathedra*, which gives a cathedral its name. The present high altar, installed in 1958, commemorates the people of the Commonwealth killed in the two world wars. The mosaics in the quire were installed as a result of Queen Victoria's complaint that the cathedral was 'most dreary, dingy and undevotional'. The sparkling mosaics made from different-sized cubes of glass, feature scenes from the Bible.

Wren insisted upon a dome for the cathedral, not a spire, which was unusual in England during the late 17th century, and this is one of the largest in the world measuring 111.3 metres (34ft) high, made from lead, and weighing 65,000 tonnes. It comprises the lantern (the highest point), the golden gallery, the brick cone, the oculus and the stone gallery. Eight pillars support the vast structure, and Wren, in his seventies, was raised up and down in a basket to check on progress.

ABOVE: Huguenot refugee Jean Tijou designed the wrought-iron Tijou Gates in the north quire aisle and most of the decorative metalwork throughout the cathedral.

•

RIGHT: The 1900 painting *Light of the World* by William Holman Hunt dominates the north transept. It depicts Christ knocking on a door that opens from the inside, symbolizing that God enters our lives only if we ask him to.

•

Wren managed to achieve the effect of the great open space he envisaged, although his original idea of using mosaics inside the dome was replaced by painted murals on the life of St Paul. The Cathedral Commissioners appointed royal artist James Thornhill (who also worked at Hampton Court Palace) who used black and white paints with exceptional cohesion. The work took four years and was finished by 1719.

ABOVE: The Whispering Gallery is 259 steps from ground level and runs around the inside of the dome. A whisper into the walls can be heard on the other side.

•

ABOVE: The dazzling view from the Whispering Gallery. To stop the dome looking like a dark funnel, Wren created the inner dome much lower than the outer.

•

RIGHT: The American Memorial Chapel with its inscription around the edge of the marble floor. A pelican in the central window symbolizes personal sacrifice for the freedom of others.

•

The baroque pair of towers on the west front was something of an afterthought by Wren. Each is topped with a pineapple, a symbol of peace, prosperity and hospitality, and were added by Wren when he was 75. Although both towers were designed to have clocks, only the south-west tower acquired one, installed in 1893, with three faces each more than 5 metres (16ft) in diameter. The American Memorial Chapel contains a roll of honour commemorating over 28,000 American servicemen and women who gave their lives during the Second World War. Below, in the south-east aisle of the crypt, lies Wren's resting place. The fitting epitaph from his son reveals, 'Reader if you seek his monument, look around you.'

THE CITY OF LONDON

One of the world's principal trading capitals, the City of London has over 500 financial institutions, buyers and brokers. Once a walled community, and still known as the 'square mile', the area comprises churches, mercantile institutions and historic remains of the old city. The City seized the opportunity for extensive rebuilding after the area was badly bombed during the Second World War. Now there is the juxtaposition of brand-new glass modernism in skyscrapers like the Swiss Re, known colloquially as the 'gherkin', with more traditional buildings such as Drapers Hall, once home to Oliver Cromwell. Views across the City can be seen from the 45-metre (142-ft) high walkway at Tower Bridge.

BELOW: Tower Bridge has become one of London's most enduring symbols. Designed by Sir Horace Jones at a cost of £800,000, it is a fantastic example of hydraulic engineering; the bascules are fully raised in just 90 seconds to allow ships through.

•

ABOVE: The dazzling Lord Mayor's Coach leads the way in November's Lord Mayor's Show.

•

BELOW: Children listen intently to a Victorian spice seller at the Museum of London.

•

Each year the City welcomes a new Lord Mayor, sworn in without saying a word during a ceremony known as the Silent Change. The spectacular Lord Mayor's show is a colourful parade harking back to 1189 when he paraded the streets, carrying a posy of flowers to allay the foul smells. The parade, with the ceremonial gold coach, starts at the 15th-century Guildhall, which lies at the centre of the square mile. Meetings and banquets are held here and the building houses banners and shields from various livery companies. The parade finishes at Mansion House, the official home of the Lord Mayor.

The Museum of London chronicles over a quarter-of-a-million years of London history in seven permanent galleries and represents the best of the city. There are over a million items and fascinating displays illustrating major moments in history, such as The Great Fire of London.

The nearby Barbican Centre, built on a Second World War bomb site, was created to provide offices, housing, shops and an arts centre. It is home to the London Symphony Orchestra, as well as to cinemas and exhibition halls.

Along Threadneedle Street is the Bank of England which was established to raise funds to fight the French in 1694, and houses the country's gold reserves. Near by, the Royal Exchange, founded in 1565, is the centre for commerce while along Lime Street is the insurance group, Lloyd's of London. The building's dynamic external structure of blue pipes and glass is spectacular when lit up at night.

Leadenhall Market, once a wholesale meat market, has now been converted into attractive restaurants and shops. The Monument, designed by Sir Christopher Wren and Robert Hooke, commemorates the Great Fire of London, symbolized by the flaming urn of copper on its top. The spectacular view from the gallery is well worth the climb!

The City and the West End are linked by Fleet Street, once synonymous with the printing presses of newspapers. Where Fleet Street meets the Strand is the neo-Gothic Royal Courts of Justice, which deals with civil, libel and divorce cases, and the four Inns of Court, where London barristers work within an intricate set of quadrangles and courtyards. Just behind Fleet Street is St Bride's Church with its wedding cake spire, built by Sir Christopher Wren in the 1680s and known as the journalists' church. The Central Criminal Court – also known as the Old Bailey after the road on which it stands – is England's premier crown court. Inside, sentence has been passed on some of the country's most hardened criminals. On top of the building stands the gold figure of Justice with a sword in her right hand and the scales of justice in her left.

ABOVE: Commemorating the Great Fire of London in 1666, the 62-metre (202-ft) high Monument is situated the same distance eastwards from where the fire started in Pudding Lane.

•

LEFT: Leadenhall Market is a thriving retail centre with cobbled walkways. In 1881 the City's architect, Sir Horace Jones, designed the present wrought-iron and glass-roofed buildings.

•

ENTERTAINMENT

ABOVE: Piccadilly Circus and Eros. The aluminium statue rises above a bronze fountain and was first unveiled in 1893. It is actually a memorial fountain celebrating the Christian Angel of Charity, not the Greek God of Love, despite many a marriage proposal beneath its wings, and commemorates the Victorian philanthropist the Earl of Shaftesbury.

•

London is liveliest in the cosmopolitan West End where a multitude of pubs, clubs, shops, theatres, wine bars and cafés compete with jugglers and buskers amidst the flashing lights and huge billboards. The mile-long Oxford Street is a shoppers' paradise of department stores, boutiques and gift shops which starts at Selfridges department store near Marble Arch tube station and stretches to Tottenham Court Road. Bissecting Oxford Street is Regent Street, home to many well-known stores, notably the fabric and artefact specialist Liberty, housed within a neo-Tudor building. A few doors down is Hamley's, one of the best-known and largest toy shops in the world. Behind these stores is the infamous sixties hippy haunt of Carnaby Street, now a paved walkway where well-known shops blend with bohemian emporiums selling everything from posters to hand-made jewellery. By continuing to the bottom of Regent Street you reach Piccadilly Circus and the Trocadero, a large family-orientated complex, teeming with restaurants, bars, cinemas, shops and Fun Land, one of the most extensive computer game arcades in London, with five floors of virtual reality. London's busy theatreland centres around the streets of Haymarket and Shaftesbury Avenue, featuring productions of the latest dramas, musicals and comedies and there are also many cafés and restaurants providing sustenance before or after the show.

ABOVE: The stunning 1821 Theatre Royal was Sir John Gielgud's 'favourite room anywhere'.

•

LEFT: Liberty's store, famous for its enchanting window displays, art nouveau interior and lush eastern carpets, houses a superb range of gifts, cosmetics and fabrics.

•

RIGHT: A selection of portrait artists vie for business around bustling Leicester Square, once home to scientist Isaac Newton and artist Joshua Reynolds.

•

BELOW RIGHT: There has been a market in Portobello Road since 1837 and today it is a popular tourist attraction, especially at weekends.

•

To the south of Bond Street, situated on Piccadilly, lies Burlington Arcade, a shopping mall dating from 1819 and designed 'for the sale of jewellery and fancy articles of fashionable demand'. It retains much of its unique character and is still an historical experience with Edwardian-frocked Beadles in top hats enforcing Regency law to ensure no-one runs or whistles!

Leicester Square is a throng of activity, illuminated at night by the multiplex cinemas bordering the central garden, which contains statues of playwright William Shakespeare and comedian Charlie Chaplin, born in London in 1889.

Away from the main tourist hub, there are bargains to be found at the many street markets around London, the best-known being Portobello Road in Notting Hill. On Saturday mornings there are many hundreds of antique stalls selling an eclectic mixture of jewellery, antiques and art. For a more contemporary feel, Camden Lock Market, overlooking Regent's Canal, attracts 150,000 people a week. Established in 1975, there are unusual and original gifts, handcrafted, traditional and fashionable jewellery, designer clothes and accessories to suit the most avant-garde. In the east end of London is Petticoat Lane market, probably the oldest of all London's street markets, dating from the 17th century when the French Huguenots sold petticoats and lace. But the prudish Victorians changed the name to Middlesex Street to avoid referring to women's underclothes! Although this remains its official designation, the old name has stuck, and the Sunday market is still known as Petticoat Lane Market. Bargain hunters can find a wide range of goods, including clothes as well as leather goods, watches and toys.

Covent Garden, once a market garden used by medieval monks from Westminster Abbey, later became renowned as London's main fruit and vegetable centre. In 1974 the market moved to Nine Elms at Vauxhall and the buildings were modernized to provide specialist shops selling crafts, jewellery and clothing. The piazza in front of St Paul's Church, known as the Actor's Church, has an abundance of street theatre, from knife jugglers, fire swallowers and uni-cyclists, to string quartets and Punch and Judy shows. On the opposite side of the square is London's Transport Museum.

ABOVE: London's Transport Museum shows how public transport has been crucial to the capital and the lives of Londoners over the past years. There are displays of horse-drawn vehicles, electric trams and vintage London buses.

PARKS OF LONDON

Kensington Gardens was created in 1689 with land annexed from Hyde Park when William and Mary became joint monarchs and moved into Nottingham House, now Kensington Palace. Today, visitors can enjoy tree-lined avenues, a flower walk, roller-blading paths and boating on the Round Pond. At the heart of the gardens, in a 1934 tea pavilion, is The Serpentine Gallery now home to contemporary art and architectural displays, and the beginning of the Diana, Princess of Wales memorial walk. A dogs' cemetery lies in Lancaster Gate to the north, created by the Duke of Cambridge in 1880 for one of his beloved pets. St James's Park, perhaps London's most pretty and ornamental park, is famous for its views towards Buckingham Palace, and its pelicans, black swans and flowers. From here you can see Westminster, St James's Palace, Carlton Terrace, Buckingham Palace and Horse Guards Parade. The pelicans originally arrived from Russia as a gift from the ambassador during the reign of James I. Today they hail from warmer climes such as Florida and are fed every day at 3pm. In the summer there are lunchtime concerts at the bandstand. Battersea Park lies on the south side of Chelsea Bridge and is marked by a Peace Pagoda erected by Japanese Buddhist monks to commemorate the Year of Peace in 1985.

BELOW: St James's Park enjoys music in the summer with concerts in the bandstand. Charles II installed an aviary along its south side, giving the street its name, Birdcage Walk.

•

RIGHT: Little Venice in Regent's Park was created by John Nash in 1820, joining the Grand Junction Canal in the west with the London Docks in the east. Originally the canal was to run through the park, until objections were raised concerning the boat owners' bad language. Today, the towpath is a lovely walk and boat trips run to Camden Lock.

•

Designed in 1811 by Crown architect John Nash for the Prince Regent, Regent's Park contains a private residential estate, Queen Mary's Gardens, Rose Gardens, a lake, a heronry and waterfowl collection. It is also home to the famous London Zoo, with over 600 species of animals including lions, tigers, primates and pandas.

LEFT: Popular with boaters, the Serpentine in Hyde Park is a delightful relaxing venue away from busy London life.

•

BELOW: The London Central Mosque was designed by Sir Frederick Gibberd and cost an estimated £6 million. The mosque holds 1,800 people under its domed roof and all visitors must remove their shoes before entering.

•

During the dissolution of the monasteries in 1536, Henry VIII used Hyde Park, part of Westminster Abbey's land, as a place for hunting. It was not until the reign of James I, in 1603, that the park, the largest open space in central London, was opened to the public. In 1851 the Great Exhibition was held here. Today, it is more famous for its lake, the Serpentine, created by George II's consort, Queen Caroline, when she decided to dam the Westbourne River in 1730. Now you can boat and swim, and listen to rousing debates at Speaker's Corner near Marble Arch. If you wish to make a point all you need is a box on which to stand and a loud voice! The tradition harks back to the Tyburn gallows when condemned men had the right to speak before execution. Hyde Park's riding track, Rotten Row, was the first public road to be lit at night and there are 6 kilometres (four miles) of horse rides as well as cycle and roller-blading routes. Classical music concerts are held here during the summer and traditional gun salutes, marking state occasions, are fired from the Parade Ground.

LEFT: Hyde Park is a great place to roller-blade and this is also becoming a fun way of getting around London!

•

45

Winding its way through the heart of London, the River Thames remains as much a part of London life now as in medieval times. The Oxo Tower, once a warehouse for a gravy-making company, has been redeveloped as exclusive apartments and a restaurant. It can be seen from Waterloo Bridge, which was rebuilt in 1939 almost entirely by women, as many of the men were fighting in the Second World War. There are skateboarders and street entertainers lining the walkway leading past the South Bank arts complex. Recognized as one of London's premier tourist attractions, the 137-metre (450-ft) high London Eye erected to mark the millennium, soars above Jubilee Gardens. Next to Westminster Bridge is County Hall, once home to the Greater London Council and now housing the London Aquarium, with a one-

RIVER THAMES

million-litre (219,974-gallon) tank containing many of the 3,500 species. The Saatchi Gallery concentrates on exhibiting art from contemporary British artists including Tracey Emin, Damien Hirst, Sarah Lucas and Jenny Saville. On the north side of Waterloo Bridge, there is the magnificent 18th-century Somerset House, originally built as government offices and now the home of the Courtauld Institute Gallery, Gilbert Collection and the Hermitage Rooms, with fabulous displays of art and silverware.

CENTRE RIGHT: The Royal Festival Hall on the South Bank was built in 1951 as part of the Festival of Britain, along with the Hayward Gallery and the National Film Theatre.

•

RIGHT: County Hall and the London Eye, with views from the top which stretch over 40 kilometres (25 miles) on a clear day.

•

LEFT: The captivating view from the Houses of Parliament down the River Thames with the spectacular London Eye landmark.

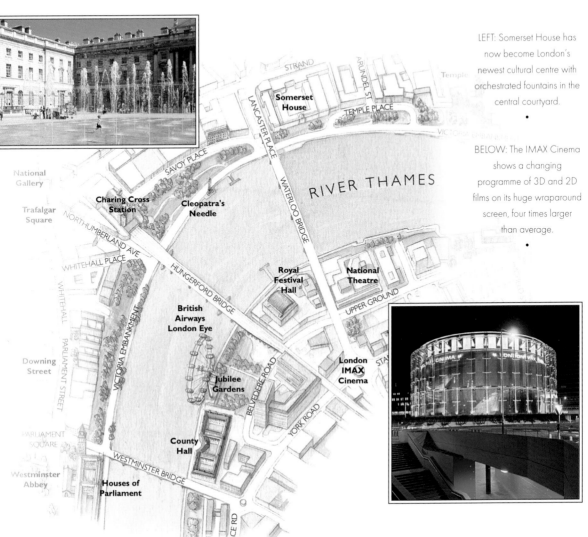

LEFT: Somerset House has now become London's newest cultural centre with orchestrated fountains in the central courtyard.

BELOW: The IMAX Cinema shows a changing programme of 3D and 2D films on its huge wraparound screen, four times larger than average.

RIVER THAMES

STRAND
ARUNDEL ST
Temple
Somerset House
TEMPLE PLACE
VICTORIA EMBANKMENT
LANCASTER PLACE
WATERLOO BRIDGE
SAVOY PLACE
National Gallery
Trafalgar Square
Charing Cross Station
Cleopatra's Needle
NORTHUMBERLAND AVE
WHITEHALL PLACE
WHITEHALL
HUNGERFORD BRIDGE
Royal Festival Hall
National Theatre
UPPER GROUND
British Airways London Eye
Downing Street
VICTORIA EMBANKMENT
PARLIAMENT STREET
BELVEDERE ROAD
London IMAX Cinema
Jubilee Gardens
PARLIAMENT SQUARE
YORK ROAD
County Hall
WESTMINSTER BRIDGE
Westminster Abbey
Houses of Parliament
PALACE RD

BELOW: The newly built
Millennium Bridge is often
better-known as the 'wobbly
bridge', because it swayed
when first opened.

RIVER THAMES

On the north side of the river the 203-tonne Cleopatra's Needle can be found on the Thames Embankment. It was presented to the British Government by Mohammed Ali, the Turkish Viceroy in Egypt as a memorial to the victories of Nelson and Abercromby over the French in Egypt. On the south side, the spacious Tate Modern converted from the Bankside Power Station for £134 million, contains contemporary British and international art.

ABOVE: The Tate Modern is
made from more than
4.2 million bricks and the
chimney was limited to
99 metres (325ft) to be
lower than the dome of
St Paul's Cathedral.

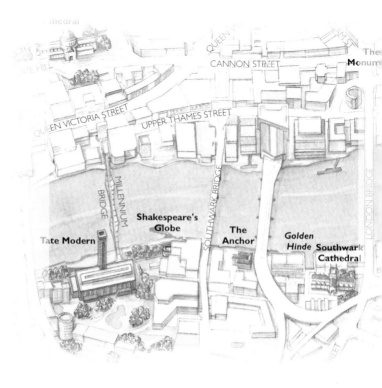